Contents

PICTURE SOURCES

Crown Copyright by courtesy of HM Postmaster-General: 15 middle, 19 lower, 21, 24 upper, 29 upper right, 30, 31 upper left and lower right, 38, 40 upper right

Horsham Museum 31 upper right

Nance Fyson: 6 left, 8, 10 left, 16 left, 25 lower, 26 all three, 32 upper, 43 lower

The Postal Museum, Bath: 11 left, 20 upper, 22 upper, 35 all four

The Post Office (Post Office copyright reserved): 9 lower, 10 right, 11 right, 12-13, 13 lower, 14 upper, 15 top, 16-17, 17 right, 22 lower, 23 left, 24 lower left and lower right, 25 upper, 29 upper left, 31 lower left, 32 lower, 33 both, 37 both, 39, 40 upper left, 41 both, 43 upper

Young Library Ltd: 6 right, 7 all three, 9 upper, 12, 13 upper, 14 lower, 15 bottom, 16 right, 17 left, 18 both, 19 upper, 20 lower, 23 right, 27, 28, 29 lower, 36, 40 lower left, 42

POST OFFICE

LETTER BOX

N° I

MILES FURLONGS YARDS

3   213

FROM THE GENERAL POST OFFICE

Do you want to write to a friend? It couldn't be easier today. You just drop your letter or card into the postbox.

Five hundred years ago people had to find their own way of sending a letter. They might have asked a traveller going in the right direction to take it. Richer people might send a servant. The Church and universities used their own messengers from one town to another.

Kings have had their own messengers since early times. By 1482, in the reign of Edward IV, special horsemen were put at a 'post' about every 20 miles/32 kilometres between London and Scotland.

These royal messengers, or 'couriers', became part of the Royal Household. Henry VIII, King from 1509 to 1547, had a servant called Master of the Posts.

From the sixteenth to early nineteenth centuries, the word 'post' meant several things. The place where a messenger stopped to change horses was a 'post'. The letter itself, and the messenger, were also called 'post'. A 'post-road' was a road on which there was a regular postal traffic.

In the late 1500s trade between Britain and Europe was growing. The road to Dover (the nearest port to Europe) had become a regular post-road. Other post-roads were set up to Ireland and Scotland.

A few private letters were allowed in the Royal Posts. However, the real

In early days the Crown and the Church had their private postal services. Here a monk hands over a sealed letter. Henry VIII (who reigned 1509-47) had a servant called Master of the Posts. Henry's portrait appears in a series of stamps on British naval history.

beginnings of Britain's public postal service came in the 1630s. Charles I wanted more money for the Royal Posts, so he allowed the public to use the service. 'The Letter Office of England and Scotland' was set up in 1635, headed by Thomas Witherings.

The official post-roads from London went to Dover, Edinburgh, Yarmouth, Chester, Plymouth, and Bristol. Letters were charged at a rate depending on the number of sheets of paper and the distance they were carried.

Two pence was charged for sending a letter up to 80 miles/129 km. Four pence was charged up to 140 miles/225 km. Any further than that within England cost six pence. Letters to Scotland cost eight pence, and it was nine pence to Ireland. A penny was a lot of money in those days. Only wealthy people could afford to use the post.

These were the charges for a single sheet of paper. If two sheets of paper were sent, the cost was double. Any

Charles I allowed the public to use his royal postal service. Letters were carried on horseback on the six main post-roads shown on the map. Then they were delivered by foot posts like the one you see here.

7

wrapper or envelope counted as an extra sheet of paper – so people hardly used them. Instead the letter sheet was folded over and sealed with a blob of sealing wax. Then the address was written on the back. You can see examples of this below and on page 10.

The postage was usually paid by the person receiving the letter, not the one sending it.

The mail was carried much the same way for the next 150 years.

The postmasters outside London were usually keepers of large inns. They kept fresh horses ready for the posts to use on the next stage of their journey. Some postmasters also delivered letters to people nearby, on horseback or foot. A 'foot post' wore a

This letter from Ireland to Kent in about 1720 shows the earliest type of postmark. It was invented by Henry Bishop, Postmaster-General. '15' in the top half of the circle, and 'SE' in the lower half, shows the letter was received by the Post Office on 15th September.

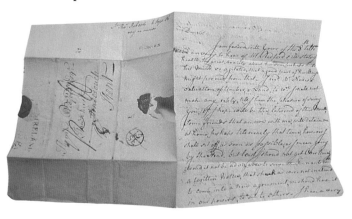

badge showing the Royal Arms while he was on duty. Both horse messengers and foot posts carried horns to let people know when they arrived.

Postboys (and a few postgirls) were in their early teens or older. There was no uniform but riders wore hats and big boots.

The new public service was an improvement, but many people were not happy. They didn't like state officials carrying their letters. They continued to use messengers and 'carriers' – men who carried goods about in a horse-drawn cart. These carriers delivered post between one tavern and another.

The official State post tried to raise the cost of sending a letter, but private competition made this impossible.

In 1653 Oliver Cromwell's government announced that the 'Office of Postage of Letters, Inland and Foreign' was to be the only carrier of letters 'in all the places of England, Scotland, and Ireland and to and from all other places within the Dominion of the Commonwealth'.

In 1657 an Act of Parliament set up the Post Office. John Thurloe was the first Postmaster-General. The Act did not allow anyone but the Post Office to carry post. But of course unofficial post continued whenever people could get away with it.

In 1660 Charles II established the General Post Office. Henry Bishop was its first Postmaster-General.

Slowly the postal service became more like the one we know today. The

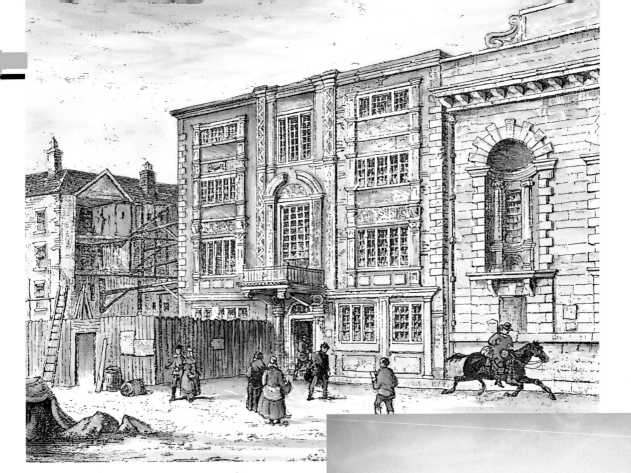

very first date-stamp was used on a letter in 1661. People had complained about letters being delayed by unreliable postboys. Date-stamping was a way of assuring people that letters were being passed on promptly.

There was a daily post to Kent and Essex. A post went every other day to other parts of England and Scotland, and every week to Wales and Ireland.

London was then very much the centre of Britain's post system. Letters came to London to be sent out again along the six post-roads of Britain. Postage was charged for the whole distance. Even a letter between two northern towns like York and Manchester went through London.

After the Great Fire of 1666 the General Post Office moved to Lombard Street. The picture at the top was drawn in about the year 1800. In 1829 it moved to a much larger building in St Martin's Le Grand, which you can see in the smaller picture.

In the seventeenth century there was no house-numbering in London. Letters were often addressed like this:

To Mr. Peter Le Neve att his house in east Hardon Street att the end of Gunpowder Alley from Shoe Lane over against the Door in the middle of the Dead Wall

The General Post Office was then in Lombard Street. This was where the Postmaster-General lived. The Post Office allowed some small shopkeepers in the City and Westminster to receive letters. The shopkeepers charged one penny a letter for receiving it and taking it to Head Office in Lombard Street.

Besides these licensed letter receivers, taverns and coffee shops helped to send and receive post. Coffee houses were especially

An 18th century letter addressed for collection at a coffee house in Chancery Lane. The postmark shows the date 9th October.

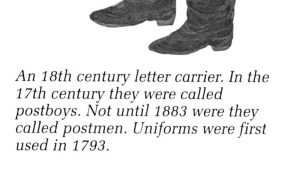

An 18th century letter carrier. In the 17th century they were called postboys. Not until 1883 were they called postmen. Uniforms were first used in 1793.

important for overseas mail, because merchants and sea captains met there to do business, and sailing dates were listed. There was a bag in each house for letters going to foreign places. People left one pence or two pence for the sea captain to take their post.

Until 1696 post could travel only on the six post-roads (see page 7). Then the first 'cross-post' was introduced – direct post between towns on different post-roads. Bristol to Exeter in 1696 was probably the first, and others followed. But these services were unofficial. In 1720 a Bath postmaster called Ralph Allen set up the first official cross-posts.

But there was still no service to small towns and villages. People living there had to pay messengers to collect their post from the nearest post-town. It was 1801 before real efforts were made to carry post to villages.

Post was moving, but a growing problem was that it wasn't safe. Postboys were often robbed. The Post Office tried using locked mail carts made of iron. Keys were given only to the postmasters.

Letter carriers of about 1800-1810. It is believed that the wooden model on the left was used as a sign outside the post office in Andover, Hampshire.

In 1702 people sending banknotes were advised to cut them in half. Each half should be sent by a separate post.

Uniforms for postboys in London started in 1793. The postboys complained that a uniform would mark them as having something to steal. But the Post Office wanted uniforms to deter postboys hanging around in ale houses.

Mail coaches were a new way of making post safer. John Palmer, a young theatre owner in Bath, came up with the plan. Each coach had a guard who sat outside at the back with the mail box under his feet. The guard wore a red coat with blue lapels and gold braid, and a black hat. He was armed with a pistol and a blunderbuss (a short gun with a wide muzzle, flared at the end). Inside the coach there was space for a few passengers.

A print of 1774 showing a mounted postboy with his great sack of mail. He has a post horn to announce his approach.

16ᴾ

SWAN WITH TWO NECKS

THE *Original* BATH Mail Coach *of 1784*

The first mail coach was tested in 1784 between Bath and London. The journey took sixteen hours. Besides being safer, the mail arrived faster. Within a few years, coaches were travelling all the main post routes.

The very first mail coach ran between London and Bath in 16 hours on 2nd August 1784.

The Holyhead to Chester mail coach trapped in snow. In the picture below, the artist has possibly exaggerated the snow's depth!

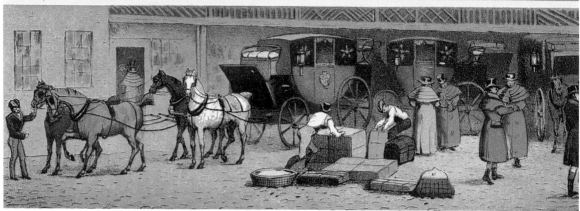

In all the time mail coaches were used, only one attempt to rob one is recorded. The coaches did face some problems, however, especially with heavy snow.

The Royal Mail did not pay tolls on the road and had right of way over other traffic. The guard blew his horn to let other traffic and toll-gate keepers know that a mail coach was coming. The other traffic had to get out of the way, and the toll-gates were flung open.

Scheduled stops were only in towns. In smaller places mail could be collected and delivered without the coach stopping at all. The guard would throw out a bag to the official letter receiver. The receiver might stand at an upper window and throw a bag to the guard, or hand it at the end of a pole as the coach dashed by.

THE EDINBURGH Mail *Snowbound in r*

Coaches for the Edinburgh route collected at the Bull and Mouth in St Martin's Le Grand. After loading up with passengers and luggage they drove to the Post Office to collect the mail. Then they departed on the Great North Road.

14

The beginning of the end of the mail coach. On 17th December 1845 the train from London completed its run to Louth. From there it was taken to Peterborough railway station, uncoupled from the horses, and loaded on to a train for the return journey.

In 1829 the General Post Office moved from Lombard Street to St Martin's Le Grand. Crowds gathered there daily, for the coaches' departure was one of the sights of London. But already their end was near. The world's first public railway had opened in the north of England four years earlier. The Post Office began using trains in 1830. In 1846 a mail coach left London for the last time.

While the General Post spread slowly across the post-roads of Britain, 'Penny Post' services grew within towns. London was where the idea began. In the mid-1600s London was already a busy place of half a million people. However, there was no official postal service within the town. A letter from one part of London to another had to be sent by servant or hired messenger.

William Dockwra's announcement of his Penny Post service. It illustrates three of the marks used to show the name of the receiving house and the time of posting. The 'L' in the triangle indicates the office in Lyme Street. The heart-shaped stamps show 8.00 in the morning, and 4.00 in the afternoon.

 The Practical Method

OF THE

PENNY-POST:

Being a Sheet very neceſſary for all Perſons to have by them,

For their Information in the Regular Uſe of a Deſign ſo well Approved of, for quickening Correſpondence, Promoting Trade and Publick Good.

With an Explanation of the following Stamps, for the Marking of all Letters.

Hereas *William Dockwra* of *London* Merchant, and the reſt of the Undertakers, (who are all Natives and free Citizens of *London*) out of a ſence of the great benefit which would accrew to the numerous Inhabitants of this Great City, and adjacent parts, (with hopes of ſome Reaſonable Encouragement hereafter to Themſelves) have lately ſet up a *New Invention* to convey Letters and Parcels, not exceeding One Pound Weight, and Ten Pounds in Value, to and from all Parts within the Contiguous Buildings of the Weekly Bills Mortality for a Penny a Letter or Parcel, whereby Correſpondency, the Life of Trade and Buſineſs, is and will be much facilitated ; and having for above a year paſt, with great pains, and at ſome Thouſands of Pounds Charge, reduced the ſame into Practice, which does manifeſtly appear to be for the Publick Good ; yet as all new

The first private bellmen appeared in 1709. The Post Office quickly closed the rival service down, but (as you see in the picture above) they copied the idea of using bellmen to receive letters. Bellmen did not disappear until the 1850s.

In 1680 William Dockwra introduced the Penny Post for letters and parcels within London. There were seven sorting houses and more than 400 receiving houses (at shops, taverns, and other small businesses) to take in the letters. Messengers called at the receiving houses every hour. Letters and parcels less than one pound in weight and worth less than £10 were delivered for one penny. The sender had to pay this cost. One new idea of the Penny Post was a postmark showing that postage had been prepaid.

London's Penny Post was very popular, but the General Post Office complained. Within about two years

The first Post Office uniform was issued to General Post letter carriers in 1793 (right). It was a scarlet coat and beaverskin hat. The picture above shows the uniform of the London District letter carrier issued in 1837.

the Penny Post was brought under the GPO's control.

A man called Charles Povey set up another system in 1709. Povey was offering to deliver letters and packages for one half penny. His 'Half-Penny Carriage' operated only in the busiest parts of London - the City, Westminster, and Southwark. Shops and other small businesses acted as receiving houses, but he also used strolling 'bellmen'. When people heard the bell ringing they brought out their letters. It saved them a visit to the receiving house.

This post office opened in Sanquhar, near Dumfries, in 1763 — and is still there!

Above is Newcastle's only letter carrier in 1821, delivering a letter to Mr H.P. Parker. Letterboxes and stamps were twenty years in the future. The other picture shows a letter carrier collecting money and giving change at the door.

Povey's service lasted only seven months. He was fined for competing with the Post Office.

However, the bellmen did not disappear. The Post Office thought the idea a good one, and continued to use it. Bellmen were seen in the streets of London until 1846. Other towns used the idea as well. Dublin used bellmen as late as 1859.

A 1765 Act allowed Penny Posts to be set up around Britain, but other towns were slow to follow London's lead. Dublin was first in 1773; then Edinburgh. Birmingham, Bristol, and Manchester opened offices in 1793.

More towns followed, but the greatest growth was during the years 1812-15. By the mid-1830s there were Penny Post offices all over Britain (295 in Ireland, 81 in Scotland, and 356 in England and Wales).

When London's Penny Post began, the sender paid the cost. By the 1790s this was not necessary. The sender could choose the method of payment, and letters were stamped 'paid' or 'unpaid'.

Collecting postage at the door took a lot of time. A letter carrier in London could deliver only a few letters per hour. The service did not reach all parts of London and other big towns.

Until 1840 newspapers, M.Ps.' 'franked' mail, and some other types of post, were carried free. The entire cost of the mail on this coach is borne by the small packet of letters.

People living in the outer districts had to collect their post from the Post Office. Postage rates were rising. In 1801 London's 'Penny' Post became the 'Two Penny' Post. The cost of General Post was going up too. In 1771 the lowest rate rose from two pence to three pence. By 1812 it cost eight pence to send a letter from London to Brighton, and thirteen pence from London to Edinburgh. People earned much less in those days so this was quite a lot of money. A working person might have to spend all they earned in a day just to send a letter.

The founder of the modern postal service — Rowland Hill. Every country in the world has copied his ideas.

History's first postage stamp! The postage stamp system was supposed to begin officially on 6th May 1840. But this letter to Peckham, in London, is date-stamped four days earlier. Nobody knows why the Bath postmaster jumped the gun.

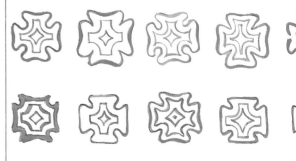

It was still common to pay on receipt. This system allowed crafty people to send messages for free. There would be a code with some word misspelled in the address or an extra word added. The receiver of the letter would study the address and read the coded message. Then he would tell the postman that, sadly, he could not afford to pay, so the letter must be sent back!

By the early nineteenth century more and more children were going to school, and learning to read and write. There was a need for a better and cheaper post system. Between 1835 and 1837 there were no fewer than five government reports about Post Office reform. Still nothing happened. Then in 1837 there appeared a historic pamphlet, which caused an immediate sensation.

Handstamps with a 'Maltese Cross' design were issued to postmasters for cancelling the postage stamps. But postmasters would sometimes lose them, and have new ones made locally. The design often varied from the original, as you can see. One of these cancellation marks may just be seen on the letter carried by the mounted postboy of 1845. Uniforms for postboys outside London were not issued until 1860, but he carries the official post horn and whip.

A replica of a 19th century post office showing pigeonholes, mailbags, scales, handstamps, and bottles of ink. It may all be seen today at the Bath Postal Museum (yes, even the cat!).

The Pamphlet was called *Post Office Reform, its Importance and Practicability.* Its author was 41-year-old Rowland Hill, a former teacher and social reformer. Hill showed that the cost of managing the Post Office

This letter posted to the Italian city of Florence needed nine 'twopenny blues' and one 'penny black' to cover the cost. Each one is cancelled with the 'Maltese Cross'.

was too high. He described how the public got out of paying postage. The franking system, giving free post to MPs and the Royal Court, was criticized as well.

People in London received post from three separate services. The Two Penny Post office handled mail within London. The Inland Office had charge of the General Post. The Foreign Office handled most of the overseas post.

Rowland Hill said it would be good sense for the Post Office to have a standard scale of charges based on weight only, not distance. And this charge should be paid by the sender. Too much time was wasted by letter carriers collecting all the different postage on letters they delivered.

As his pamphlet explained:

There would not only be no stopping to collect the postage, but probably it would soon be unnecessary even to await the opening of the door, as every house might be provided with a letter box into which the letter carrier would drop the letters, and, having knocked, he could pass on as fast as he could walk.

Rowland Hill suggested three ways a letter could be pre-paid. The sender could either:

1. pay cash to a clerk at the Post Office;

2. buy specially marked paper or envelopes; or

3. buy labels to stick on to the envelope or stationery. They would act as a receipt to show that payment had been made.

An 1890 printed envelope and a 1979 stamp, both commemorating the introduction of the penny post in 1840.

An alternative to postage stamps was the official printed envelope. As it was sold by the Post Office for one penny, it did not need a penny stamp. This design by William Mulready did not last long because many people mocked it. Others liked to colour the picture before posting. The letter to Malta (posted in Bristol on 14th November 1840) had to carry stamps as well, to cover the extra postage for overseas mail.

Everyone agreed it was a good idea to pay for postage before the letter was sent. The question was, which way of prepaying was best? A public contest was held. A prize of £200 was offered for the best idea. Over 2,600 designs and suggestions were made. Only 49 of these talked about adhesive postage labels (which later came to be called postage stamps).

The earliest design for a postage stamp seems to be from James Chalmers, who was a Dundee bookseller. In 1837 he wrote a letter suggesting little gummed slips of paper. They could be printed in sheets, and then cut apart as needed. They could be 'cancelled' by being stamped with the town's name and the date, to prevent them being used a second time.

The stamp this forgetful old gentleman is looking for is the 'penny red' which replaced the penny black after only nine months.

The design eventually chosen was sketched by the artist Henry Corbould. The Queen's head was used, as it was very familiar.

The new stamps were printed in black - the famous 'penny black'. There were 240 stamps on a sheet, divided by a narrow margin to allow for cutting apart with scissors. It was not until 1854 that perforated sheets became common. Henry Archer's invention for perforating meant the stamps could easily be torn apart instead of cut. An alternative to the adhesive stamp was the 'embossed' design.

This beautiful valentine made of silk and lace is mounted on a postcard. Cheap postage made valentines enormously popular.

25

Left: A pillarbox at Bishop's Caundle, Dorset, placed there in late 1853. Not quite the oldest in Britain – two at St Peter Port, Guernsey, were in use by February that year. The other two boxes were introduced in the 1860s, and can still be seen in various parts of Britain.

These 1970 stamps feature three 'first issues' of the 1840s and 1850s. The shilling green stamp was the first embossed issue; the one penny black was the first engraved stamp; and the four pence carmine was the first to be surface printed.

It was on 1st May 1840 that the Penny Post and the world's modern postal system was born. The new stamp and envelopes went on sale to the public. The official date set for their first use was 6th May but a few were sent earlier.

Queen Victoria liked the stamp very much. The same young face was used right through her long reign. The only words on the stamps were 'Postage One Penny'. Even today, all British stamps show the head of the current King or Queen. They are the only ones in the world that do not have the country's name printed on them.

The idea of using envelopes became quite popular. Until the 1840 reforms, putting a letter inside an envelope meant paying higher postage (the envelope counted as an extra 'sheet'). Letters had simply been folded over, sealed, and the address written on the back.

The new envelopes were not gummed. They were sealed by sealing wax or by small coloured wafers. Attractive designs and mottoes were printed on the envelopes.

William Mulready designed an envelope and letter sheet issued in 1841. The public thought it too

Four stamps issued in 1977 to commemorate the Queen's 25 years on the throne.

serious and some cartoon envelopes became popular instead.

Christmas cards were used for the first time in 1843. Cheap postage, and the use of envelopes, made these cards popular. The golden age of the lover's valentine also began in the 1840s. Many of these valentines used embossed paper and lace. Before 1840, the high cost of postage caused poorer lovers to leave their valentine at a sweetheart's door.

Anthony Trollope, a famous novelist, was also a Post Office surveyor. He had the idea for postboxes. The first postbox was placed in Jersey in 1852. Postboxes were used on Britain's mainland for the first time in 1853. People no longer had to travel to the post office every time they wanted to post a letter.

A woman in one of Trollope's novels was worried about the new 'iron boxes' as many other people were. She could not see why people should put their letters into an 'iron stump' (as she called it) in the middle of the street. There was no one there to look after them!

Two ways of picking up mail at speed.
Above: handing mail to the Bath
coach as it travels at 13 kph in the
1780s. Right: the 1934 Irish Mail's
travelling post office collects a mail
sack at nearly 100 kph.

London's first pillarbox was placed in
1855 at the corner of Fleet Street and
Farringdon Street. Not until 1859 was
the shape and colour of postboxes
standardized throughout the country.

POST OFFICE
LETTER BOX
Nº 1
MILES FURLONGS YARDS
3   213
FROM THE GENERAL POST OFFICE

In the 1850s, boxes of various designs were ordered by District Surveyors for their own areas. But nine years later, boxes were made standard for the whole country. Each was marked with a 'VR' design (Victoria Regina, which means Queen Victoria). The mark changes each time a new king or queen comes to the throne, but 'VR' boxes can still be seen.

Most postboxes are now red, the royal colour. Before 1874, most boxes were dark green. People thought these looked drab and were hard to spot. It took ten years to re-paint boxes red all over the country.

Wall letter boxes – boxes set into a wall – were first used in 1857. In country areas there appeared small boxes fixed to a post. The original, free-standing boxes came to be known as pillarboxes.

By 1841, less than a tenth of letters were being posted unpaid. People welcomed the idea of prepayment. The next step was to say that all letters

A river postman of about 1910 delivering letters to ships in the Port of London.

In Horsham in the 1880s the postman went his rounds on an extraordinary five-wheeled pedal cycle. It soon became known as the Hen and Chickens. This is a replica in Horsham Museum. The bicycle cart below was used in the 1920s.

Mail coaches returned to British roads when the parcel post began in 1883. The photo (about 1898) shows parcels going 'up' (towards London) from Hounslow and Windsor. The painting (a few years later) shows a coach going 'down' to Guildford.

There have always been people who like to decorate their envelopes. On the one postmarked 8th July 1889 the address is incorporated in the rhyme. The envelope going to an Epsom address is a valentine posted in Hong Kong in 1875.

should be stamped. It was 1853 when people first had to use stamps in most of Britain.

The penny black was really too good a stamp. The black ink was so permanent that the red cancellation mark could be taken off by a solvent. This allowed people to re-use the stamps. After only nine months the Post Office changed from the penny black to the penny red.

Over the years new values and designs of stamps have been added.

'Definitives' are permanent issue stamps that show mainly the King or Queen's head and a number value. Commemorative stamps have become very popular. They celebrate occasions such as a royal marriage, the Olympic Games, or the anniversaries of historical events.

Cheaper postage in 1840 was only the start of many changes for the Post Office. Deliveries were made more days of the week and more times per day. By 1864 nearly 95 per cent of letters were delivered right to the door. However, it was not until 1897 that delivery was guaranteed to every address in Britain.

Uniforms for letter carriers had been extended to the London Two Penny Post in 1837. These London carriers wore blue coats with red lapels. General Post carriers still wore red. Larger towns began having uniformed carriers in 1856. In 1862 the General Post uniforms changed from red to blue. Rural carriers started wearing uniforms in 1872.

One useful reform before 1840 was an 1829 plan to speed up deliveries to outer districts of London. Letter carriers had been collecting their bags from the General Post Office in central London, then walking several miles to the beginning of their routes. Now special horse-drawn carriages called 'accelerators' carried fourteen men at a time. Each man got off when the carriage came near his route.

The Post Office had been using the railway since 1830. The first 'travelling post office' (TPO) ran between Birmingham and Warrington in 1830.

A TPO is a carriage in which the sorters work as the train moves. At first there was no way of delivering mail bags while the train travelled at speed. The train had to slow down so that bags could be thrown out on to the station platform. Later, the bags were dropped down a chute, but the train still had to slow down. From 1848 a net was fixed at the side of the track to catch the mail sacks as the train thundered past.

You can always tell in which reign a post box was erected because the monarch's initial appears on it (followed by 'R'; see glossary). The full-length pillarbox shows Edward VII (who reigned 1901-11). The close-up shows his grandson George VI (who reigned 1936-52).

The Post Office also used boats. Since 1800 the River Post has been delivering letters and parcels to ships in the Port of London.

As the Post Office grew it still faced some competition. Private firms were fined for doing what was, by law, only for the Post Office. In 1887 a company called Boy Messengers set up in London, offering speedy delivery of letters. In 1891 the Post Office set up the Express post service as a way of meeting the competition.

The Post Office monopoly did not cover parcels. Several private road carriers and railway companies were busy carrying parcels around the country. In 1848 the Post Office started its book post service. All books, newspapers, and other printed papers could be sent, in open covers, at a special lower rate.

A regular parcels service at last began in 1883. All of the 15,000 post offices had to be fitted out for sorting parcels. Letter carriers had their walks changed so that loads would not be too heavy. The name letter carrier was changed to postman.

The Post Office tried all sorts of handcarts and large baskets. Bicycles were first used in the 1880s, almost as soon as they were invented. They were in common use by 1900.

In 1887 the Post Office went back to using mail coaches on certain routes. These coaches travelled at night and carried no passengers. The only Post Office employee on the coach was the guard. He carried a sword and revolver. By the First World War, in 1914-18, a fifth of all parcels were carried by road. It was less during and after the war.

Horse-drawn vans were used in London to carry mail to and from the main railway stations. The change to using motor vans came slowly. In 1920 the Post Office bought fifty light motor vans to use in rural areas. The next year another 300 motor vans were ordered. It was 1949 before the last horse-drawn mail van was off the streets of London.

The penny post lasted for many years. The basic rate for most inland letters stayed at one penny from 1840 to 1918. It was only the weight that changed. In 1871 the weight allowed for one penny went up from half an ounce to one ounce. In 1897 it went up to four ounces.

The First World War started in 1914. Postage was seen as a way of raising money for the war effort. The weight carried for a penny went back to one ounce. There was no more penny post after 1918. The lowest rate was one-and-a-half pence, and this went up to two pence in 1920.

Four postcards of the First World War (1914-18). 1, A 'field service' card on which a soldier was allowed only to cross out unwanted phrases, to prevent useful knowledge possibly falling into enemy hands. 2, A sentimental message for a father at the front. 3, An appeal to write to soldiers far from home. The artist Donald McGill was famous for a very different type of postcard which can still be seen at seaside resorts! 4, One of a series called 'Our Fair War Workers'.

NOTHING is to be written on this side except the date and signature of the sender. Sentences not required may be erased. If anything else is added the post card will be destroyed,

I am quite well.

I have been admitted into hospital.

{ *sick* } *and am going on well.*

{ *wounded* } *and hope to be discharged soon.*

I am being sent down to the base.

                              letter dated ....

I have received your { *telegram ,,* ....

                              parcel ,, ...

Letters follows at first opportunity.

I have received no letter from you.

{ *lately.* }

{ *for a long time.* }

Signature } *Bob*
Only.

Date *22/7/15*

(Postage must be prepaid on any letter or post card addressed to the sender of this card.)

There's lots of things I'd like to say,
But don't know how to write,
I pray God keep you every day,
And guard you every night.

Love to my dear Daddy

WHEN THIS YOU SEE—

REMEMBER ME!

Billie.

35

60th ANNIVERSARY of the FIRST
SCHEDULED UNITED KINGDOM
INTERNATIONAL AIR MAIL SERVICE
Folkestone-Cologne

1 March 1919

FLOWN FROM ROYAL AIR FORCE NORTHOLT ON THE
60th ANNIVERSARY OF THE START OF THE U.K. FIRST
REGULAR INTERNATIONAL AIR MAIL TO KÖLN-BONN,
COMMEMORATING THE FLIGHTS MADE ON 1st MARCH
1919 FROM RAF HAWKINGE TO KÖLN-MERHEIM.

CAPTAIN: FLT. LT. P. R. ELDER, RAF.

NAVIGATOR: FLT. LT. J. M. GREENLAND, RAF.

ON BOARD: BRIGADIER J. BRIDGE, RE
Director of Postal and Courier Services.
MR. TERENCE CUNEO.

AIRCRAFT: D.H. DEVON C1, VP 976 OF No. 207 SQN.
RAF NORTHOLT.

FLIGHT TIME: 2 HOURS.

Group Captain
W S O Randle
Poste Restante
Cologne

The Post Office did not only deliver letters and parcels. Since early times it had offered other services. Money orders began as early as the 1790s. It was not safe to send cash through the post. Instead a person who wanted to send money could go to a post office and buy a voucher called a money order. The order stated the name of the person buying it, and the person and office where it could be exchanged for cash.

The Post Office Savings Bank began in 1861. In 1880 came the idea of

The first official air mail in Britain was carried from London to Windsor in September 1911. At the foot of this postcard (right) the Postmaster-General disclaims responsibility for any delay! The first regular international air mail (from Folkestone to Cologne in Germany) in March 1919 is commemorated by the first day cover (above) issued sixty years later. The poster (far right) is advertising air parcel post to the continent. By the end of the 1920s there was a regular service as far as India.

recording the amount saved by sticking stamps on a card. This way of saving small amounts at a time was very popular with children. Schools Savings Banks were started, and by the early 1900s were in more than one-third of junior schools.

Old age pensions began in 1908, and national insurance in 1911. The Post Office had a key role in the new welfare schemes. Pensions were paid out at post offices, and insurance stamps were sold there. The Post Office became more and more the local office of the State. By 1922 it was even selling licences to keep dogs or guns.

The first postcards appeared in 1869 in the Austro-Hungarian Empire, but other countries soon took up the idea. The first British postcards went on sale in 1870. They could be sent for a half penny postage. At first they were just plain, buff cards for the address to be written on one side and the message on the other. When picture postcards appeared the message had to be written on the same side as the picture. It was not until the early 1900s that the address and message could be on the same side.

Picture postcards became very popular. They had views of beautiful scenery and historical buildings. There were comic cards with jokes as well – by the 1930s some of these were very vulgar!

In the early 1900s the post was very much quicker than it is today. A woman could post a card to her butcher in the morning for an order of meat to be

delivered that afternoon! Many towns had six post deliveries a day in 1903. This was down to four deliveries a day by 1914.

For many years overseas letters had been sent as 'ship letters' or 'packet letters'. A ship letter was given to the captain of a private vessel who took it to a port in return for a small charge set by the Post Office. A packet letter was sent on a government ship.

A train with no passengers or crew – just mail. The Post Office has operated this underground railway since 1927. The photos show the earliest and the latest type of trains.

Britain's trade with other countries was expanding. People were leaving Britain to set up home in the colonies. More and more people wanted to send letters overseas, and a campaign began for cheap ocean postage. In 1847 the cost of sending a letter overseas from Britain had been twelve pence. In 1911 postage to anywhere in the British Empire cost just one penny.

In 1870 the telegraphic service became part of the Post Office. In 1912 most private telephone systems became part of the Post Office as well. By the beginning of the First World War in 1914, the Post Office employed over 250,000 people. Most of them were postal workers.

The amount of post had grown enormously. So had the traffic, and it was a problem to move the post fast enough through the streets of London. One idea was for an underground railway.

Some trials had been made in the 1860s and 1870s with mail going through underground pneumatic tubes, but nothing came of that. A tunnel for an underground railway was started in 1914 but was delayed because of the war. The Post Office (London) Railway finally opened in 1927. Now called Mail Rail, it is the only one of its kind in the world. Six sorting offices are linked with the main railway stations at Paddington and Liverpool Street.

Mail Rail has twenty-three miles of track, seven stations and thirty-four trains that travel at 56 kph. The trains are operated by remote control. No drivers, guards, or passengers travel on

FOR PARTICULARS SEE AIR MAIL LEAFLET
OBTAINABLE FREE AT THE COUNTER
IMPERIAL AIRWAYS
THE ONLY BRITISH AIR LINE TO THE CONTINENT

Imperial Airways carried mail to many places overseas in the 1920s and 1930s. The black-and-white photo shows a Post Office 'streamline van' beside a mail-carrying passenger plane at Croydon Airport in 1935. In the 1980s colour photo mail is being put aboard a British Airways jet.

this underground. The largest platform is at the Mount Pleasant station. The sorting office above this station is the largest in the world.

Aeroplanes were first used to carry mail in 1911, the year George V was crowned. The pilot was Gustav Hamel. Carrying just one bag of post, Hamel left from Hendon and landed near Windsor Great Park fifteen minutes later.

The first regular air mail service was started between London and Paris in 1919. By 1934 U.K. air mail post was 122 tons a year.

Imperial Airways began in 1924 to carry mail overseas. The service extended to India by 1929 and to Australia by 1934. A British North Atlantic air mail service began in 1939, but was soon interrupted by the Second World War (1939-45).

Air mail is now used to carry post within Britain as well as overseas. The first air mail without any special air fee

Remember your house now has a postcode.

Postcodes were introduced in 1970 to assist the electronic sorting of mail.

was in 1934 between Inverness and Kirkwall. In 1979 a Flying Royal Mail service was started.

In 1939, the beginning of the Second World War caused shortages. The Postal Museum in Bath has an envelope that was re-used twelve times. When one penny stamps were in short supply in 1940, some two penny stamps were cut diagonally. Each half was used as a one penny stamp.

There were shortages of planes as well, because planes were needed for the war. There was not enough space for air mail. The answer was the 'airgraph'. The sender of an airgraph wrote a letter on a special form. This was

photographed and reduced. It was possible to put 1600–1700 messages on a 30-metre reel of film weighing only 140 grammes. At the end of the flight the film was printed and enlarged. The message could then be placed in an envelope and delivered like an ordinary letter.

Airgraphs were for the Armed Forces only at first, and cost three pence each. In 1942 they became available to the public for eight pence each. More than 61 million airgraphs were delivered in 1942, and 135 million the following year.

The Post Office issues licences for all sorts of activities. This poster is reminding people they must have a licence to watch TV. It no longer costs only £3.00 – this was in 1957!

41

These four stamps were issued in 1985 to celebrate 350 years of postal services. 350 years since what, exactly? You can remind yourself by looking back to page 7.

Another way of sending a message was by telegram. The telegraph service had been taken over by the Post Office in 1870. Early telegrams were often used for bad news, such as deaths or accidents, so most people were frightened to receive a telegram.

In 1935 the Post Office began a greetings telegram service. A golden envelope showed that the news inside was good. The greetings were printed on decorated printed forms. 'Nine words for nine pence' was the greetings telegram rate.

Greetings telegrams were very popular, and by the 1980s they greatly outnumbered other telegrams. The telex and telephone were used more for serious news. As the demand for telegrams had been declining, the service was ended in 1982.

A very important change in the last forty years has been the growing use of machines to do jobs that were once done by hand. The use of post codes, begun in 1968, greatly speeds up the job of sorting. The first part of the code indicates an area such as a town, or part of a large town. The second part of the code refers to a very small number of addresses – an average of seven addresses per code. The sorter taps the code on to a keyboard, and the machine does the rest.

Letters could be sorted by hand at the rate of 2,000 per hour. But 16,000 an hour could be sorted by automatic sorting machine. Soon we expect machines to be sorting 30,000 letters per hour.

The Post Office delivers about 54 million letters per day to about 24 million addresses. At Christmas it delivers about 1.5 billion letters, cards, and parcels. One day's mail laid end to end would reach to the North Pole and back. Five days' mail would stretch around the equator.

In 1981 the postal and tele-communications services were separated. The department dealing with telephone and telex was named British Telecom. British Telecom became a private industry in the mid-1980s. There have been suggestions to make the Post Office a private industry too. Many people do not like this idea. Some Post Office services cannot make a profit. For example, sub-post offices in villages, and delivery of post in rural areas, lose the Post Office over £30 million a year. A private industry might decide to cut out these services.

Five hundred years ago most people couldn't read or write. Other people hardly ever sent letters because it was too costly. Today, mail is an important part of life for most people.

The history of Britain's post is the story of how it has become easy and cheap for us all.

Her Majesty's Post Office will deliver every letter in Britain to the recipient's door, no matter how remote it may be. Few other countries offer this service.

Try to visit a postal museum. They are a fascinating source of social history. This one, in Bath, is on the site of the 1840 post office which issued the first postage stamp anywhere in the world.

BATH POSTAL MUSEUM

GLOSSARY

bellman: a man who rang a bell in the street to announce he was available to collect post for delivery.

cancellation: a mark stamped on to a postage stamp to prevent its re-use.

Charles I: King from 1625 to 1649 who founded the first public postal service.

Charles II: King from 1660 to 1685 who founded the General Post Office.

Cromwell, Oliver: ruler of England between the reigns of Charles I and Charles II, who banned private competition with the state postal system.

cross-posts: roads connecting the main post-roads.

date stamp: a postmark applied to show the time and date of receipt at the post office.

Dockwra, William: founder of the first Penny Post service in 1680, and the inventor of postmarks indicating prepayment of postage.

emboss: to mark an envelope with a stamp which raises parts of the paper's surface into a particular design.

first issue: a postage stamp of a denomination or design which has not appeared before.

foot post: an unmounted postman of the 17th and 18th centuries.

frank: an official mark on an envelope to show that it may travel free (or that postage has already been paid).

General Post Office (GPO): the official name of the national postal service.

Great Fire: a fire which destroyed most of the City of London in 1666,

Hill, Rowland: founder of the modern postal service, who introduced postage stamps and a uniform postage rate.

letter carrier: the term for a foot postman before 1883.

mail: a batch of posted letters or parcels.

packet boat: a ship authorized by the GPO to carry mail overseas.

penny post: the basic rate for general post from 1840 to 1914.

Penny Post: various private services for delivery of post within cities between 1680 and 1840.

postage: the fee for a postal delivery. A postage stamp is a sticky label showing that postage has been prepaid.

postboy: a man or boy who carried post on horseback.

postman/postwoman: the person who delivers the post to the door (called letter carrier until 1883).

postmark: a stamped mark which shows the post office and date of posting, or acts as a cancellation.

Postmaster-General: the official head of the GPO.

post office: a local office of the GPO whose main task is to receive post and collect postage.

post-road: one of the main roads upon which post was carried.

R: the letter which on postboxes follows the initial letter of the monarch's name. It stands for the Latin words Regina (Queen) and Rex (King).

seal: a piece of wax (usually impressed with an identifying mark) used to fasten together the edges of a piece of folded paper.

stamp: a tool which applies an inked or embossed impression on to a piece of paper.

telegram: a written or typed copy of a telegraph message.

telegraph: a communication system which sent coded electric signals down a wire to a receiving unit.

travelling post office (TPO): a coach on a train in which mail is sorted, and from which mail is collected and delivered at stations along the route.

INFORMATION

PLACES TO VISIT

National Postal Museum, King Edward Street, London EC1A 1LP, tel. 071 239 5420. Stamps of Great Britain and the rest of the world; temporary exhibitions on philatelic and postal subjects. Lecture theatre/cinema, and shop.
Postal History Collection, Bruce Castle, Lordship Lane, London N17 8NU, tel. 081 808 8722.
The Postal Museum, 8 Broad Street, Bath BA1 5LJ, tel. 0225 460333. Of special interest to families and school groups; includes life-size model of 1840s post office. Activities room, video room, and library for mature students. (Admission charge.)
The Story of Telecommunications, 145 Queen Victoria Street, London EC4V 4AT, tel. 071 248 7444 or freephone 0800 289689. History of telecommunications, which was the concern of the Post Office until 1981. Lecture theatre/cinema, resource centre, and shop.
Stanley Gibbons Ltd, 339 Strand, London WC2R 0LX, tel. 071 836 8444. World's largest stamp shop has stamps, historical covers, books, albums, and catalogues at pocket-money prices. Other stamp shops in Britain may be found under 'Stamp Dealers' in Yellow Pages.

For adult students

Post Office Archives, Mount Pleasant Sorting Office (entrance in Phoenix Place), London EC1A 1BB, tel. 071 239 2570.
BT Archives, Room G09, Telephone House, 2-4 Temple Avenue, London EC4Y 0HL, tel. 071 822 1002. Telecommunications history only.

BOOKS

Let's Go to the Post Office, F. Peacock (Watts)
Letter - Where Does it Come From?, Kathy Henderson (MacDonald)
Post, V. Pitt (Watts)
Postman, T. Ford (Wayland)
Postmen, D. Smith and D. Newton (Schofield & Sims)
Postmen and the Post Office, H. Adams (Blackwell)
Story of the Post, R. Page (Black)
Story of the Penny Black, A.G. Rigo de Righi (National Postal Museum) for mature readers.

FILMS AND VIDEOS

The Post Office Film and Video Library offers free loan of a wide range of documentary and educational material. Subjects include Post Office history, careers, Britain in the 30's and 40's, and philately. Free catalogue from P.O. Box 145, Sittingbourne, Kent ME10 1NH, tel. 0795 426465.

OTHER RESOURCES

The Post Office Education Service will provide a wide variety of material, some without charge. These include books, computer programmes, videos, and National Curriculum Guidelines for most Post Office resources. Free catalogues from P.O. Box 145, Sittingbourne, Kent, ME10 1NH, tel. 0795 426465

INDEX